RELIGIOUS LIBERTY IN THE UNITED STATES MILITARY

CHRISTOPHER T. INO

…unless the LORD guards the city, the watchman keeps awake in vain.

— Psalm 127:1

Contents

Introduction

The General hopes and trusts, that every officer and man, will endeavour so to live, and act, as becomes a Christian Soldier defending the dearest Rights and Liberties of his country.

— George Washington, General Order, July 9, 1776

How far have we fallen? How far have we come from being able to issue a general order exhorting the men to be Christian Soldiers? The state now thinks religious liberty is subordinate to government interests. The term *religious liberty* is lip service that fills empty regulations to appear accommodating. Religious liberty is now code word for pluralism, not worshiping and following Jesus Christ according to our conscience.

Many Christians who are in the military are torn over their service to the Lord and service to their country. On one hand, the thought of a military as powerful as ours devoid of moral men frightens them. On the other, the military is going down a road that asks them to do things against their consciences. We struggle because we do not want to surrender such a strategic institution to secular humanists; we know that leads to tyranny.

In this field manual, we will consider your religious rights in the US military. We will begin at the beginning when God spoke the creation into existence, move down through our wonderful Christian heritage as found in the US Constitution, then land on current military regulations. The option for Christians who have run into a situation that goes against their conscience is to submit a waiver or potentially submit an affidavit to their commander if they are receiving unlawful orders. This needs to be conducted wisely, so we will consider Christian conduct through the process and practical preparations.

It is absurd that a waiver must be approved by the state. The situation may seem dire. But take heart; Jesus Christ is King of kings and Lord of lords. All authority on heaven and earth has been given to Him (Matthew 28:18). He is the LORD strong and mighty, the LORD mighty in battle (Psalm 24:8). He is the LORD of host…Yahweh of armies.

Bibliography

1. John Clement Fitzpatrick, ed., *The Writings of George Washington, from the Original Manuscript Sources 1749-1799*, vol. 5, 7-9-1776. Washington D.C.: United States Government Printing Office, 1931-1944.

1

God-Given Authority and Blessings

Why are the nations in an uproar and the peoples devising a vain thing? The kings of the earth take their stand and the rulers take counsel together against the LORD and against His Anointed, saying, "Let us tear their fetters apart and cast away their cords from us!" He who sits in the heavens laughs, the Lord scoffs at them. Then He will speak to them in His anger and terrify them in His fury, saying, "But as for Me, I have installed My King upon Zion, My holy mountain." "I will surely tell of the decree of the LORD: He said to Me, 'You are My Son, today I have begotten You. Ask of Me, and I will surely give the nations as Your inheritance, and the very ends of the earth as Your possession. You shall break them with a rod of iron, you shall shatter them like earthenware.'" Now therefore, O kings, show discernment; take warning, O judges of the earth. Worship the LORD with reverence and rejoice with trembling. Do homage to the Son, that He not become angry, and you perish in the way, for His wrath may soon be kindled. How blessed are all who take refuge in Him!

– Psalm 2

THERE IS ALWAYS MUCH TALK ABOUT *RIGHTS*. PEOPLE talk about human rights, civil rights, unalienable rights, universal rights, or religious rights. When talking about *rights*, the first distinction that needs to be made is that *blessings* (not rights) are from the Triune God of the Bible and not from the government or some universal declaration; there is no such thing as *rights*. This doesn't change when you are in the military. The Triune God of the Bible is the God of armies...and economics, politics, sports, schools, families, and so forth. This needs to be kept in mind when seeking to exercise your religious freedoms. We tread on dangerous ground when we seek *approval* from government rather than for them to *acknowledge* this blessing. You already possess religious freedoms as given by God in Christ Jesus our Lord, and governments are responsible to God to acknowledge that blessing. This chapter is going to look at authority as it is laid out in the Bible and the blessed freedoms we have in King Jesus.

Creation

The doctrine of a literal seven-day creation is very weak among modern Christians. At worst, Christians disregard Genesis 1 and fall into the foolishness of evolution. However, more often than not, Christians try to reconcile Genesis 1 with the *theory* of evolution, and yes, it is a theory, not science. They have come up with the Gap Theory, the Day-Age Theory, or Progressive Creationism, all of which fall short of what the Bible teaches. That needs to change. We need to return to believing what the Bible says: that God is Creator, and we are His creatures. The Creator–creature distinction is foundational to understanding everything and anything. As the creature, we need to acknowledge who made us and understand it is God who made things the way they are (Isaiah 45:9; Romans 9:21). It is God who created all things seen and unseen. It is God in His providence who upholds the created order, who some would wrongly call "nature" (Genesis 1; Hebrews 1:3; Job 38:33–37; Colossians 1:16–17). As the Creator of the heavens and the earth, He has all authority and He has delegated some of that authority to humans and human institutions.

Ultimate Authority

In the Gospel of Matthew prior Jesus' accession, He says, "All authority has been given to Me in heaven and on earth" (28:18). The Triune God of the Bible is the only holder of absolute authority. All other authorities established in the Bible are given limits. Gary DeMar in his book *God and Government: A Biblical, Historical, and Constitutional Perspective,* he begins his chapter on biblical authority by stating, "God is the ultimate and only independent authority. He is the Sovereign Creator who controls time and history. He establishes authority and deposes those who fight His absolute sovereignty" (pg. 421).

Biblical Governments

As the Creator of all things, God has established in His Word different governing bodies. They are self-government, family government, ecclesiastical (church) government, and civil government. Each of these governments has been given limits to its sovereignty and is responsible to God to stay within those boundaries. Foundational to family, church, and civil governments staying within their bounds is the idea of self-government. Individual people need to submit to King Jesus and follow Him. Unless there are God fearers (self-government) in these institutions, they will refuse to submit to the Creator who has given them their authority. DeMar warns what will happen when governments do not serve the Triune God:

Without an ultimate authority established by an unchanging and sovereign God, all earthly authorities vie for ultimacy and set standards for themselves and ultimately for other people. When the Triune God is rejected as the source and dispenser of authority and power, we can expect cooperation between various authorities to cease and competition, and eventually conflict, to prevail. The most powerful authorities then work to eliminate what they perceive to be their competition. The State is the most powerful authority in terms of temporal punishment; it has the power of the sword. When it sees itself as ultimate and independent of God, all other authorities (e.g. families and churches) are no longer viewed as allies but competitors. Their authority must be eliminated. Children no longer belong to parents and therefore must be educated by the State, to be called in service for the State. Churches can teach 'religious' doctrine so long as that teaching does not address issues that are controlled by the State. (*God and Government*, pg. 423)

Due to the depravity of man, we are prone to go beyond the limits God has set for us. After Adam fell in the garden, man has been a slave to sin. We became slaves to our lusts for power, the desires of the flesh, and all forms of unrighteousness (Romans 6). The *only* way to be free from sin is through Jesus Christ. Without Christ, you will have a pagan society, and all pagan societies eventually lead to an authoritarian civil government.

Family, church, and civil governments can all overstep their bounds. The matter of the family and church will not be talked about in this book, but we will talk about self-government in chapter 4 on Christian virtue. We will now turn our attention to civil government.

Civil Authority

Christians are not to be anarchists or revolutionaries. Civil governments are legitimate authorities established by the Triune God. "Every person is to be in subjection to the governing authorities. For there is no authority except from God, and those which exist are established by God" (Romans 13:1; also see 1 Peter 2:13; Titus 3:1). If the ditch on the left side of the road is anarchy, then the ditch on the right side of the road is misunderstanding these verses to mean blind submission. The Christian is not to fall into either of these ditches.

It seems that Christians inherently know that if an authority (parents, husbands, church leaders, military leaders, civil magistrates, etc.) commands them to murder someone (Exodus 20:13) or to not preach the gospel (Acts 5:29), they are to obey God rather than man. This is an easy first distinction. If somebody commands you to break God's Law, you are to disobey, and in disobeying that authority, you are obeying God. But what if the civil government regulates how often a church can celebrate the Lord's Supper? Or if they order the church not to gather on Sunday? Can the church execute a convicted murderer? Can the civil government tell you what you must wear, what you must inject into your body, who you can or cannot sell goods to? The problem being brought up is not a matter of whether a murderer should be executed or whether someone can tell you what to wear. The problem is *who has the authority to do so?*

The civil magistrate has been given the ministry of the sword. They are granted the authority to punish the evildoer as defined by God's Law. The civil magistrate is sent by God "for the punishment of evildoers and the praise of those who do right" (1 Peter 2:13); "…it is a minister of God, an avenger who brings wrath on the one who practices evil" (Romans 13:4). It is important to note what evil is and what good is. Evil cannot be defined by utilitarianism, social contract, cultural relativism, or some other ethics. Evil can only be defined by the Creator, the Triune God, our ultimate authority. It may be thought that isn't true for the civil government if they don't acknowledge the Triune God or if they espouse a pluralistic society. This is seen in our government as they misunderstand the First Amendment and twist history by saying "separation of church and state." It is agreed that there is a separation of church government and state government, but it should never be understood as a separation of God and government. The civil government is to be in submission to God's Law as found in the Word of God. DeMar lays out additional duties of the civil magistrate:

> The additional duties of the civil government are the well ordering of society and the maintaining of peace so that Christians are free to worship God, unhindered by forces hostile to the gospel of Jesus Christ. The State has the duty to preserve law and order so that the Church is free to spread the gospel of peace. The civil government must be made to realize that there is no real peace without the presence of the Spirit of Jesus Christ. This climate of peace can only be accomplished by administering justice and righteousness. Justice and righteousness are defined in terms of God's law. Civil rulers are commissioned to represent God as the Judge. They act in such a capacity when they punish those who do evil (i.e. break God's laws), as well as publicly commend those who do good (cf. Romans 13:3–4), (*God and Government*, pg. 74).

What happens when the civil government commands something outside their authority? The question of how Christians should answer this in general alone requires at least a book. There already is a rich tradition on Protestant Resistance Theory, and some of these titles will be in the bibliography. But for the Christian military member, this means submitting a religious waiver to claim your religious freedoms in Jesus Christ as granted by the Triune God. If the government is causing harm in the way of giving unlawful orders, this may call for submitting an affidavit to the commander issuing the unlawful orders.

Blessings

Christians do not believe in human rights or civil rights or some idea of universal rights. We do not have a right to life, liberty, property, or happiness…all of which are blessings. We believe the wages of sin is death (Romans 6:23); thus, you don't have a right to life, but deserve death. We were slaves to sin (Romans 6:17); thus, we don't have a right to claim liberty. We don't have a right to property, happiness, or blessings apart from obedience to Christ, and even here, obedience does not necessarily mean material blessings. We only have liberty in Jesus Christ. The liberty that we are used to in the United States is the *fruit of the gospel of Jesus Christ*. Those freedoms will go away in a society that apostatizes.

Greg Bahnsen writes in *Theonomy in Christian Ethics*, "Having redeemed us from the curse of the law, Christ gives us the freedom we need: ethical ability to keep God's law in grateful love to Him – not the commonly urged type of 'freedom' which turns God's grace into licentiousness (Jude 4)" (pg. 467). All of this was realized by our founders. The words of John Adams capture this well: "Our Constitution was made only for a moral and religious people. It is wholly inadequate to the government of any other."

Bibliography

1. Bahnsen, Greg. *Theonomy in Christian Ethics.* Nacogdoches, TX: Covenant Media Press; Third Edition, 2002.

2. Brutus, Junius. *Vindiciae Contra Tyrannos: A Defense of Liberty Against Tyrants.* Moscow, ID: Canon Press, 2020.

3. DeMar, Gary. *God and Government: A Biblical, Historical, and Constitutional Perspective.* Powder Springs: American Vision, 2011.

4. New American Standard Bible, 1995.

5. Rutherford, Samuel. *Lex, Rex: The Law and the King.* Moscow, ID: Canon Press, 2020.

6. Sunshine, Glenn. *Slaying Leviathan: Limited Government and Resistance in the Christian Tradition.* Moscow, ID: Canon Press, 2020.

2

Constitutionally Acknowledged Rights

*I go further and affirm that bills of rights, in the sense and to the extent in which they are contended for, are not only unnecessary in the proposed Constitution but **would even be dangerous**. They would contain various exceptions to powers not granted; and, on this very account, would afford a colorable pretext to claim more than were granted. **For why declare that things shall not be done which there is no power to do?** Why, for instance, should it be said that the liberty of the press shall not be restrained, when no power is given by which restrictions may be imposed? I will not contend that such a provision would confer a regulating power; **but it is evident that it would furnish, to men disposed to usurp, a plausible pretense for claiming that power.** They might urge with a semblance of reason that the Constitution ought not to be charged with the absurdity of providing against the abuse of an authority which was not given, and that the provision against restraining the liberty of the press afforded a clear implication that a power to prescribe proper regulations concerning it was intended to be vested in the national government.*

– Alexander Hamilton: Federalist No. 84

THIS QUOTE FROM ALEXANDER HAMILTON DISPLAYS the debate around the ratification of the Bill of Rights. His worry was that if we added a Bill of Rights to the US Constitution, it would cause confusion because we the people, through the US Constitution, did not grant the federal government the authority or power in any of these areas. Imagine if you gave power of attorney to a friend to sell your car, but added an amendment saying, "You cannot sell my house." It would be strange to add that because you never granted those powers. Although the Bill of Rights was eventually ratified, the original intent was never to say that these rights are granted by the government to its people. As we delve into this chapter, I do not want you to forget that there is only liberty and blessings in Jesus Christ. Ultimately, it is not a "bill of rights" that grants freedoms to Christians and societies.

The question I want to consider in this chapter is: *Does the US government acknowledge military members as having the same freedoms under the Bill of Rights as civilian citizens?* Unfortunately, this doesn't play out as a simple black-and-white answer. There has not to my knowledge been a Supreme Court case dealing with the military in relation to the First Amendment Free Exercise Clause. In Justice Douglas' dissenting opinion in *Parker v. Levy* (1974), he says, "But the cases we have had so far have concerned only the nature of the tribunal which may try a person and/or the procedure to be followed. This is the first case that presents to us a question of what protection, if any, the First Amendment gives people in the Armed Services: 'Congress shall make no law…abridging the freedom of speech, or of the press'" (417 U.S. 733, 768). We will be looking at *Parker* in this section, but it specifically deals with freedom of speech, or of the press, not with "prohibiting the free exercise thereof." Additionally, we will consider more recent Supreme Court case rulings even though they do not deal directly with military members.

Parker v. Levy (1974)

Parker is set during the time of the Vietnam War. An Army doctor was convicted of violating Articles 90, 133, and 134 of the Uniform Code of Military Justice (UCMJ). The doctor disobeyed an order to establish a training program for Army Special Forces (Art. 90), and he made public statements to black enlisted men to refuse their orders to fight in the Vietnam War and called Special Forces "liars and thieves," "killers of peasants," and "murderers of women and children" (Art. 133&134). One facet to consider in this case was the primacy of "freedom of speech" vs. "conduct unbecoming an officer and a gentleman" (Art. 133) and "all disorders and neglects to the prejudice of good order and discipline in the armed forces" (Art. 134). Now before moving on, I do not think the slanderous speech of this doctor displays Christian virtues, but that will be a topic addressed later. In the majority opinion of *Parker*, it is stated:

> While the members of the military are not excluded from the protection granted by the First Amendment, the different character of the military community and of the military mission requires a different application of those protections. The fundamental necessity for obedience, and the consequent necessity for imposition of discipline, may render permissible within the military that which would be constitutionally impermissible outside it. Doctrines of First Amendment overbreadth asserted in support of challenges to imprecise language like that contained in Arts. 133 and 134 are not exempt from the operations of these principles...This Court has, however, repeatedly expressed its reluctance to strike down a statute on its face where there were a substantial number of situations to which it might be validly applied. Thus, even if there are marginal applications in which a statute would infringe on First Amendment values, facial invalidation is

inappropriate if the "remainder of the statute...cover a whole range of easily identifiable and constitutionally proscribable... conduct..." (417 U.S. 733, 758 & 760).

The dissenting opinion states:

So far as I can discover the only express exemption of a person in the Armed Services from the protection of the Bill of Rights is that contained in the Fifth Amendment which dispenses with the need for "a presentment or indictment" of a grand jury "in cases arising in the land or naval forces, or in the Militia, when in actual service in time of War or public danger." By practice and by construction the words "all criminal prosecutions" in the Sixth Amendment do not necessarily cover all military trails. (417 U.S. 733, 766).

What do we make of this? First, military members do enjoy the protections granted in the Bill of Rights. Second, there is some precedent that the "freedom of speech" as found in the First Amendment is "marginally infringed" on by Articles 133 and 134 of the UCMJ. One of the distinctions brought out in the court ruling was not so much what the doctor said, but the context around what he said. He didn't make these comments at an "Army wives' tea party." He made these comments at his hospital, on duty, to enlisted personnel, and in the presence of patients and those performing duties under his immediate supervision. However, the dissenting position did not believe First Amendment rights to free speech should be infringed upon. Finally, there is nothing in this ruling to suggest the free exercise of religion is infringed upon.

Roman Catholic Diocese of Brooklyn v. Cuomo (2020)

Roman is set in the context of the COVID-19 time frame. In New York, Governor Andrew Cuomo signed Executive Order 202.68 creating restrictions on religious services in "red zones" and "orange zones." The boundaries for these zones were constantly changed by the governor. For example, if you fell within the boundaries of the red zone, a house of worship could only have 10 persons present, and if you fell within the orange zone, you were capped at 25 persons. At the same time, "essential" businesses were allowed to admit as many people as they wished. Examples of "essential" businesses included things like "acupuncture facilities, camp grounds, garages…plants manufacturing chemicals and microelectronics and all transportation facilities."

During this time, the Roman Catholic Diocese of Brooklyn and Agudath Israel of America submitted applications for injunctive relief challenging these restrictions based on the Free Exercise Clause of the First Amendment. The court ordered in favor. Justice Gorsuch said, "Government is not free to disregard the First Amendment in times of crisis. At a minimum, that Amendment prohibits government officials from treating religious exercise worse than comparable secular activities" (592 U.S. 1, 1 (2020)). That is a clear statement.

Religious Freedom Restoration Act of 1993 (RFRA)

Based on *Roman Catholic Diocese of Brooklyn v. Cuomo*, it would be easy to conclude that if a law doesn't intend to discriminate against religion, then as long as it is equally applied, it would be legal. But this is not the case; our religious right is "preferred." The RFRA found in its congressional search that "laws 'neutral' towards religion may burden religious exercise as surely as laws intended to interfere with religious exercise." In a survey of religious freedoms starting from the earliest days of the American colonies to *Employment Division v. Smith* (1990) and following, Thomas Jipping and Sarah Parshall Perry state:

> These precedents provided the elements of the Supreme Court's approach to free exercise cases. 1. The standard of review must be based on the "preferred" character of the right to exercise religion and the burden on that right – rather than the government's purpose or objective in imposing that burden. 2. Religion-neutral statutes or regulations may place unconstitutional burdens on the exercise of religion. The fact that it may appear facially nondiscriminatory, as the Court said in *Murdoc* [v. Commonwealth of Pennsylvania], is "immaterial." 3. While not providing an absolute shield for particular religious practices or government actions, the strict-scrutiny standard does mean that government may not burden the exercise of religion any more than absolutely necessary.

> As Justice Sandra Day O'Connor put it: The compelling interest test effectuates the First Amendment's command that religious liberty is an individual liberty, that it occupies a preferred position, and that the Court will not permit encroachment upon this liberty, whether direct or indirect, unless required by clear and compelling governmental interests "of the highest order."

However, in 1990, the Supreme Court ruled in *Employment Division v. Smith* (1990) in a manner that went against decades of First Amendment interpretation in many cases. Justice Antonin Scalia wrote that so-called "neutral laws" are obligatory for citizens even if they "incidentally" burden the exercise of religion. This reversal of the historic understanding of the First Amendment had major effects. Jipping states:

> While the application of strict scrutiny did not result in widespread religious exemptions, abandoning that standard [the traditional understanding of the First Amendment] had immediate and dramatic effect. Less than two years after *Smith*, a Congressional Research Service report documented federal and state court decisions rejecting religious exercise clams of all kinds...Simply put, applying "the principle of non-exemption stated in *Smith* has resulted in the denial of most free exercise claims."

This short history gives us the context leading up to the Religious Freedom Restoration Act of 1993. *Smith* "virtually eliminated the requirement that the government justify burdens on religious exercise imposed by laws neutral towards religion." The RFRA restored the government's requirement to provide *compelling justification* if it tries to abridge the free exercise of religion.

Conclusion

We saw in this chapter that from the earliest days of the US Constitution, the Bill of Rights was never intended to imply the government has the right to abridge religious freedoms. In fact, the Preamble acknowledges that liberty is in fact a blessing. It needs to be noted that there is a huge jump in thought moving from those early days to the arguments laid out in the Supreme Court cases. Even the idea that the government can abridge those rights with *compelling justification* is novel. With that being said, we saw in *Parker v. Levy* that the Bill of Rights still applies to members of the US military. However, there is precedence from that case that the freedom of speech can (in very limited ways) be infringed upon. In *Roman Catholic Diocese of Brooklyn v. Cuomo*, we saw that even in a time of crisis, the government is not free to disregard the First Amendment. Finally, by looking at the Religious Freedom Restoration Act of 1993, we saw that our religious rights are "preferred." We saw that even seemingly "neutral" laws may not burden our "preferred" right as found in the First Amendment. With the advent of the RFRA, we will now look to see how this law affected military regulations.

Bibliography

1. *Employment Division v. Smith*, 494 U.S. 872 (1989)
2. Jipping, Thomas & Perry, Sarah. *The Religious Freedom Restoration Act: History, Status, and Threats.*
3. The Heritage Foundation, May 4, 2021. http://report.heritage.org/lm284
4. *Parker, Warden v. Levy*, 417 U.S. 733 (1974)
5. Religious Freedom Restoration Act of 1993, Report 103–111, 103rd Congress, 1st Session, July 27, 1993
6. *Roman Catholic Diocese of Brooklyn v. Cuomo*, 592 U.S. 1 (2020)

3

Military Regulations

[T]he DoD Components will accommodate individual expressions of sincerely held beliefs (conscience, moral principles, or religious beliefs) which do not have an adverse impact on military readiness, unit cohesion, good order and discipline, or health and safety.

— DoDI 1300.17 para 1.2.b (September 1, 2020)

WE HAVE BEEN LOOKING AT RELIGIOUS LIBERTY FROM large to small. We started with our ultimate authority in the Triune God, the Creator of the heavens and the earth, of all things visible and invisible. From there, we moved to the US Constitution in general, then looked to see if there were any nuances for the military. From the US Constitution, we looked at public law. We will now zoom in to military regulation. Due to pressure from lawmakers in the time frame of COVID-19, the US military brought its religious liberty regulations in line with the Religious Freedom Restoration Act of 1993 (RFRA). Twenty-seven years after the passage of the RFRA, on September 1, 2020, Undersecretary of Defense for Personnel and Readiness Matthew P. Donovan approved DoD Instruction 1300.17, *Religious Liberty in the Military Services.*

Individual Expression Clause

With the liberalization of the Christian church, it may be difficult to find unified support for biblical principles. For example, the Roman Catholic Church disapproves of vaccines that have used fetal cells from elective abortions, but they offer a caveat. They say if there is no other option, it is morally justifiable to use them. If a Roman Catholic military member thinks it is sinful to participate in vaccines that have used fetal cells in the design and development, the production, and/or the confirmatory lab tests, they may feel they have no backing. However, the Individual Expression Clause grants them protection. The Federal Register, Volume 82, *Federal Law Protections for Religious Liberty* says:

> The Free Exercise Clause protects not just the right to believe or the right to worship; it protects the right to perform or abstain from performing certain physical acts in accordance with one's beliefs. Federal statutes, including the Religious Freedom Restoration Act of 1993 ("RFRA"), support that protection broadly defining the exercise of religion to encompass all aspects of observance and practice, *whether or not central to, or required by, a particular religious faith. (emphasis added).*

It should go without saying, but Christians should not just make things up to express themselves. Our consciences should be bound by the Word of God as found in Holy Scripture. With that being said, we will move to examining sincerely held beliefs.

Sincerely Held Belief Clause

In DoDI 1300.17, under the heading of "sincerely held belief," it has the categories of conscience, moral principles, or religious belief.

How is it that Christians have sincerely held beliefs? The answer to that begins the same way as the first chapter of this book: The Triune God created all things. Therefore, all truth only makes sense within the context of the Christian worldview. That statement requires unpacking; however, it is too lengthy for this book. Read the works of Cornelius Van Til and Greg Bahnsen, as they have dealt exhaustively with that subject. Because of this, all things—the *true, good,* and *beautiful*—ultimately belong to the Triune God and are therefore religious. To believe otherwise is to fall into the myth of neutrality.

The call from unbelievers to "be neutral" and to find the "common ground" are not neutral statements. If they deny that "the fear of the LORD in the beginning of knowledge" (Proverbs 1:7), they are not neutral; they are enemies of Christ. That is not a neutral position. Unbelievers like to pretend they are neutral; however, they are not neutral, and you shouldn't be either. In the book *Always Ready,* Greg Bahnsen states in the chapter titled "The Immorality of Neutrality":

All the *treasures* of wisdom and knowledge are to be found in Christ; thus, if one were to try and arrive at the truth apart from commitment to the epistemic authority of Jesus Christ he would be *robbed* through vain philosophy and deluded by crafty deceit (see Col. 2:3–8). Consequently, when the Christian approaches scholarship, apologetics, or schooling he must staunchly refuse to acquiesce to the mistaken demand of neutrality in his intellectual life; he must never consent to surrender his distinctive religious beliefs "for the time being," as though one might thereby arrive at genuine knowledge "impartially." The *beginning* of knowledge is the fear of the Lord (Prov. 1:7). Attempting to be neutral in one's intellectual endeavors (whether research, argumentation, reasoning, or teaching) is tantamount to striving to erase the antithesis between the Christian and the unbeliever. Christ declared that the former was set apart from the latter by the truth of God's word (John 17:17).

There is no such thing as neutrality; everything is religious in nature. The question shouldn't be whether something is religious, but which religion does it serve? Does it begin with the fear of the LORD? If not, then who is the god of that worldview? You find their god when there is no longer a higher court of appeals. For example, if you believe that the Supreme Court is the final arbiter of truth, then your god is the state. So what constitutes a "sincerely held [religious] belief" for the Christian? Everything found in God's Word. Everything found in the created order that is *true, good, and beautiful.* It does not get much simpler. Anything in defense of the Word of God is a sincerely held belief. Anything in defense of truth is a sincerely held religious belief. Van Til is credited with saying that "the Bible is authoritative in everything it speaks about, and it speaks about everything."

Compelling Governmental Interest/Justification

From the last chapter on constitutionally acknowledged rights, we saw decades of legal precedence acknowledging that the government must have *compelling justification* in order to infringe on the Free Exercise Clause. In *Employment Division v. Smith*, we saw Justice O'Connor, quoting from *Wisconsin v. Yoder*, say, "The compelling interest test effectuated the First Amendment's command that religious liberty is an independent liberty, that it occupies a preferred position, and that the Court will not permit encroachment upon this liberty, whether direct or indirect, unless required by *clear and compelling governmental interests 'of the highest order'"* (*Smith* 494 U.S. 872, 895; emphasis added). This should cause us to immediately ask the question: *And when did the government decide it owns that caveat?* Who defines *clear, compelling,* and *highest order*? If the government defines them, then that is a conflict of interests. If the government defines them and uses that authority to infringe on the Free Exercise Clause, then that seems like the government presupposes it is in its authority to do so. Don't forget Alexander Hamilton's comment on the Bill of Rights from Federalist No. 84. As we digress into how the military defines *compelling justification,* let us not forget these points.

DoDI 1300.17 para 1.2.e says, "DoD Components have a compelling governmental interest in mission accomplishment at the individual, unit, and organizational levels, including such necessary elements of mission accomplishment as military readiness, unit cohesion, good order and discipline, and health and safety." That section goes on to talk about how DoD Components will normally accommodate by excusing service members from policy, practice, or duty and can only deny them their First Amendment rights if: "(1) The military policy, practice, or duty is in furtherance of a compelling governmental interest" and "(2) It is the least restrictive means of furthering that compelling governmental interest." Finally, the burden of proof displaying that a religious exemption meets the reasons for denial is placed on the DoD Component, not the individual requesting an exemption. *This means the DoD owes service members a written response stating how their requested exemption conflicts with a compelling governmental interest and for them to display how they are using the least restrictive means in accomplishing the mission.*

Mission Accomplishment Clause

We now come to the Mission Accomplishment Clause, which includes, but is not limited to, military readiness, unit cohesion, good order and discipline, and health and safety per DoDI 1300.17. Unfortunately, that same regulation does not define any of those terms, other than providing subcategories for mission accomplishment. In order to get the most overarching idea of the US military mission, we will turn to the 2018 National Defense Strategy.

In former Defense Secretary Jim Mattis' summary of the 2018 Nation Defense Strategy, he opens by saying, "The Department of Defense's enduring mission is to provide combat-credible military forces needed to deter war and protect the security of our nation." Through the rest of the summary, he lays out what he thinks this means. First, he talks about the global strategic environment, then lays out the DoD objectives. Finally, he talks about the military's strategic approach to "provide combat-credible military forces," which includes: (1) building a more lethal force, (2) strengthening alliances and attracting new partners, and (3) reforming the department for greater performance and affordability.

At this point, we run into some difficulty. From the National Defense Strategy down to a member's unit, there will probably be multiple layers of command, who each have their own mission. Each unit mission should be able to tie back to the National Defense Strategy, but individual circumstances cannot be addressed here. However, as a side note, if an individual unit actually has a compelling government interest that conflicts with a religious conviction, perhaps the military would consider reassignment or reclassification (e.g., see DAFI 52-201 para 2.7).

The military has some difficulty here as well. As talked about in the section preceding this, the burden of proof resides with the DoD Component (per DoDI 1300.17 para 1.2.e.) to prove that a religious conviction conflicts with the mission. This can cause judgments from commanders to be subjective. We will consider an example to demonstrate this.

To continue the example used earlier, let us assume there is a Christian who objects to taking a vaccine that has used aborted fetal cells in the design and development, the production, and/or the confirmatory lab tests. A commander cannot just say, "Such-and-such regulation says it's required for your medical readiness, and medical readiness affects mission accomplishment; therefore, it's a compelling government interest that you get the vaccine." This is the logical fallacy *petition principii*, or begging the question. It is a fallacy of form that assumes the thing that needs to be proven. In this example, "such-and-such regulation" is the thing assumed that needs to be proven. Rather, the military must objectively demonstrate how not getting a vaccine impacts mission accomplishment. This cannot be theoretical or merely say "it affects the health and safety of you, the unit, and the organization." How it affects health and safety must be truthfully and objectively demonstrated.

Other Topics

The remainder of the topics in DoDI 1300.17 will only be mentioned. The regulation deals with two other major topics: responsibilities and processing accommodation requests. The section on processing covers topics such as: timelines for approval, approval authorities, the appeals process, and more. It is highly recommended that military members read through this regulation if they are seeking a religious waiver, regardless of them already being in the military or considering joining. Additionally, it is highly recommended that those seeking a waiver look at their service-specific regulations, as they might be helpful. For example, the Air Force's DAFI 52-201, *Religious Freedom in the Department of the Air Force,* has some additional language. In para 2.1, it says, "...only impose limits on such expressions when there is a real (not theoretical) adverse impact...." This additional language ensures the Air Force does not use theoretical reasons for denying a religious waiver. In para 2.7, it gives options to seek reassignment, reclassification, or voluntary separation if a request cannot be approved. And in para 2.11, it exempts members from compliance regarding "medical practices" and "immunizations" if members are seeking a waiver in those categories. Do your homework and get into the regulations.

Conclusion

In this section, we examined DoDI 1300.17 para 1.2.b, "[T]he DoD Components will accommodate individual expressions of sincerely held beliefs (conscience, moral principles, or religious belief) which do not have an adverse impact on military readiness, unit cohesion, good order and discipline, or health and safety." We saw that *individual expression* of a sincerely held belief does not necessarily mean it has to be your denomination's view. We saw that *sincerely held belief* is anything found in God's Word or defending the true, good, and beautiful in His creation. We saw that it is the government's responsibility to demonstrate that a policy, practice, or duty is actually (not theoretically) in the furtherance of a *compelling governmental interest* in the context of *mission accomplishment.* From here, we will move on to considering some practical preparations when submitting a waiver.

Bibliography

1. Bahnsen, Greg. *Always Ready: Directions for Defending the Faith*. Nacogdoches, TX: Covenant Media Press, 1996.
2. Department of Defense Instruction (DoDI) 1300.17. *Religious Liberty in the Military Services*. September 1, 2020.
3. Department of the Air Force Instruction (DAFI) 52-201. *Religious Freedom in the Department of the Air Force*. 23 June 2021.
4. *Employment Division v. Smith*, 494 U.S. 872 (1989)
5. Federal Law Protections for Religious Liberty; 82 Fed. Reg. 49668 (October 26, 2017).
6. Mattis, Jim. *Summary of the 2018 National Defense Strategy of The United States of America: Sharpening the American Military's Competitive Edge*. https://dod.defense.gov/Portals/1/Documents/pubs/2018-National-Defense-Strategy-Summary.pdf.

4

Christian Virtue

To sum up, all of you be harmonious, sympathetic, brotherly, kindhearted, and humble in spirit; not returning evil for evil or insult for insult, but giving a blessing instead; for you were called for the very purpose that you might inherit a blessing. For the ones who desires life, to love and see good days, must keep his tongue from evil and his lips from speaking deceit. He must turn away from evil and do good; he must seek peace and pursue it. For the eyes of the Lord are towards the righteous, and his ears attend to their prayer, but the face of the Lord is against those who do evil. Who is there to harm you if you prove zealous for what is good? But even if you should suffer for the sake of righteousness, you are blessed. And do not fear their intimidation, and so not be troubled, but sanctify Christ as Lord in your hearts, always being ready to make a defense to everyone who asks you to give an account for the hope that is in you, yet with gentleness and reverence; and keep a good conscience so that in the thing in which you are slandered, those who revile your good behavior in Christ will be put to shame.

— 1 Peter 3:8-16

IT WOULD BE OF NO BENEFIT IF A CHRISTIAN WERE seeking a religious waiver while not acting like a Christian. In fact, it would probably do more harm than good. In this section, we will consider your conduct as a military member. This includes not only your conduct during the process of working toward a waiver, but also the type of man you are when conducting your day-to-day activities.

The Good Man

Is your life inconsistent with your Christian profession? Are you going out to the strip club with the guys on the weekend? Are you getting hammered when you are on training trips? Is your speech in the team room replete with curse words and sexual jokes? Are you unfaithful to your wife? Do you participate in any sort of fraud, waste, or abuse? Do you neglect the gathering of the saints to worship on Sunday? If the answer is yes to any of the above, perhaps some repenting is in order. These are all small things that you are called to be faithful in. These are some of the "basics" that you need to master in obedience to Christ. If you cannot be faithful with a little, more than likely, you will not be faithful with a lot. If you are not faithful in small tests, more than likely, you will not be faithful with the large tests.

It is of the utmost importance, whether you're in the military or not, to work out your own salvation. The apostle Paul says you were "created in Christ Jesus for good works" (Ephesians 2:10). James says, "faith, if it has no works, is dead, being by itself" (James 2:17). You need to bear fruit in keeping with repentance (Matthew 3:8; Luke 3:8; Acts 26:20). "[Y]ou were formerly darkness, but now you are Light in the Lord; walk as children of Light (for the fruit of the Light consists in all goodness and righteousness and truth) trying to learn what is pleasing to the Lord" (Ephesians 5:8–9). It is true that the chief end of man is to glorify God and enjoy Him. However, this isn't the only reason to pursue virtue. The apostle Peter said, "Keep your behavior excellent among the Gentiles, so that in the thing in which they slander you as evildoers, they may because of your good deeds, as they observe them, glorify God in the day of visitation" and "For such is the will of God that by doing right you may silence the ignorance of foolish men" (1 Peter 2:12, 15). Do not give the military reason to question your *sincerely held belief* in the Triune God.

Many modern Christians think this section is the end of the story. They think that being a "good" man makes us righteous and faithful, but this is not the case.

Good at Being a Man

A Christian man must be good at *being* a man. How is that for an inflammatory statement in this day and age? Prior to the fall of humanity into sin, "[T]he LORD God took the man and put him into the garden of Eden to cultivate it and keep it" (Genesis 2:15). There are many applications that can be taken from this verse. There is an implication that man is to work, worship, protect, guard, and more in the garden. God intended for Adam, as an image bearer, to imitate Him (1:27). He was to separate (guard/keep) the garden from things outside the garden (2:15) as God separated light and darkness (1:4), the waters above and below (1:7), and the land from sea (1:9). He was to fill the earth (1:28) as God filled the heavens with lights (1:14), the oceans with creatures, the skies with birds (1:20), and the land with beasts (1:24). He was to name (speak) the animals as God spoke the creation into existence (1:3; 2:19).

Work is good and is given to us by God. It is important to note that work came before the fall and is not a result of sin. In your vocations, you are to be a man on a mission, working as to the Lord and not man (Colossians 3:23). You need to humbly work toward becoming a master of your trade. All too often,

Christians think all they need to do is have a daily quiet time, to read their Bibles, to pray an hour a day. In doing so, they neglect their responsibilities. They become sluggards and weak. That is false piety. Men are to be protectors and providers. They are to be strong with their muscles, morals, and mind. Men should be leaders displaying confidence, being competent, and being consistent in their actions.

When you are interviewing with the chaplin to see if your beliefs are sincerely held, they probably won't consider this category. They want to see if you actually believe what you say and if your conduct is consistent with what you say. But commanders see your actions, and if your work sucks, they will know. You ruin your credibility in the general sense as to why you should be in the military in the first place. Don't suck at being a man.

The Christian Man

What do you do with this information? It is possible to be a "good" man and not be good at being a man. This is the effeminate man (1 Corinthians 6:9). As you look at that verse in your Bible, you'll notice that certain translations have intentionally left that word out, but it is there in the Greek. A man who is effeminate is in sin and needs to repent. There is an example of this where a Christian implied that if his wife were being assailed, he would not defend her. He states multiple reasons for this. However, he is failing to keep (protect) his garden (Genesis 2:15). This person sounds like a good Christian by talking about the love of Christ, that Christ died for that criminal and so forth; however, he is effeminate and sinful.

There is also the possibility of being good at being a man, but not being a good man. This is the immoral man. There is a good chance you know the type. An example is the guy you would follow into the worst battles but would not want to bring around your family. He is probably the guy who is strongest in the gym and who can ruck 10 kilometers with 100 pounds through rough terrain and still be worth his salt on target. He is the man who understands the enemy and knows the best tactics to win battles. He is the man who is depended on at work because he gets things done. But unfortunately, he is also immoral. He sleeps with a different woman each weekend. He regularly gets hammered drunk. Maybe he is taking steroids to give him a leg up. And he is proud of it all.

Christian men are to be good men who are good at being men. Be competent in your vocation but also be a moral man. The apostle Paul sums it up: "Be on the alert, stand firm in the faith, act like men, be strong" (1 Corinthians 16:13).

Conclusion

You need to make yourself indispensable to the military. If the military chooses to get rid of you, it should hurt them to lose such a good solider. Most of all, you want to please Christ in your conduct.

Bibliography

1. Conn, Eric. *Hard Men Podcast: Biblical Masculinity in a World of Softness.* (various podcasts)
2. Foster, Michael and Tennant, Bnonn. *Its Good to be a Man.* (various articles)
3. Garris, Zachary. *Masculine Christianity*. Ann Arbor, MI: Zion Press, 2020.
4. New American Standard Bible, 1995.
5. Renn, Aaron. *The Masculinist.* (various articles)

Preparing for Battle

Now these are the nations which the LORD left, to test Israel by them (that is, all who had not experienced any of the wars of Canaan; only in order that the generations of the sons of Israel might be taught war, those who had not experienced it formerly).

– Judges 3:1-2

HOW DID WE GET TO WHERE WE ARE? THERE ARE those who have been Christians their whole lives, then maybe a policy changed in the military that goes against their conscience or maybe some information they didn't know about comes to light. There are those who became Christians while in the military, then maybe they realized something was wrong as they grew in Christ. Whether your story is like one of these or something different, we will cover some practical preparations.

Church

Hebrews 10:25 says, "...not forsaking our own assembling together, as is the habit of some, but encouraging one another…" Being well integrated into your local church cannot be stressed enough. Appearing before the Triune God to worship is commanded of you, and that should be enough. God is gracious though, in that going to church to worship also blesses you. I do not want you to think only in terms of "what can I get out of this," but we will consider some of the blessings here. First, being part of a community of believers who support you in seeking to obey God is very important. Depending on what you are seeking a waiver for, it can be a lonely road. Perhaps you are not allowed on base and are forced to take leave, immediately isolating you from your coworkers. Perhaps the word gets out and your coworkers are gossiping about you…and so forth. You need to be part of a community. Second, you need to be seeking godly counsel. Your pastor and elders should know what's going on with you, and if not, you need to tell them. The Proverbs say, "For by wise guidance you will wage war, and in abundance of counselors there is victory" and "Prepare plans by consultation, and make war by wise guidance" (24:6; 20:18). Do not do this in a vacuum; go to church and worship God.

Homework

You have probably heard many times in the military that "nobody cares about your military career as much as you do." Apart from a few exceptional leaders I have crossed paths with, this tends to be true. Also, if you are already reading this, this may be a moot point. Either way, you need to be reading every applicable regulation. I assure you, commanders and the judge advocates will not give you all your options. Whether this comes from malicious intent or incompetence is for God to know. Either way, as you saw in the chapter on military regulations, there is a lot there that is beneficial to you. You need to know if your chain-of-command is deviating from the regulations so you can *gently* help them course correct. Do not forget your Christian virtue in this process. Although the Bible does not directly address this situation, it does address pastors correcting older men, and the principle applies here. First Timothy 5:1 says, "Do not sharply rebuke an older man, but rather appeal to him as a father." It can be easy to get angry when you know something is being done incorrectly to your detriment, but exercise some self-control and work through it with a level head.

Antifragility

The military is a strange beast in that it seems antifragile. You are going to get paid regardless of a pandemic or recession. You will have a lifetime pension and lifetime health insurance if you retire. It is all secure…until it isn't, until they try to force you to do something against your conscience. Suddenly, you realize that you are completely dependent on the government. The government gives you money for clothes, money for shelter, money for food, and so forth. They give you everything you need, as long as you obey. In another context, that might sound like slavery. There is a real chance this military has given you skills that don't really matter. You can operate an M-240B as if it were part of your body, program a radio, or follow a checklist. Those skills don't translate very well outside the military.

Although this could have been talked about in the section on masculine Christian virtue, it's relevant here too: You need to be building skills. This is part of being good at being a man. In addition to building your skills as they pertain to your job in the military, you should be pursuing other skills as well. In the book *Durable Trades: Family-Centered Economies That Have Stood the Test of Time,* author Rory Groves lays out 61 trades that have lasted for centuries. He also analyzes our economy in general, starting from before the industrial revolution leading up to the present. He shows how work has moved away from the home, and this has created wage slaves and broken the family, among other things. We no longer look at the home as a place to be productive and a place to pass culture and values to our children, but a place for relaxation and entertainment.

You should start looking at how you and your family can be productive in the home. This does not have to be anything large but can start very small. One of the simplest things you can do is learn how to grow your own food and how to preserve it after harvest. Perhaps you can try raising chickens for meat and some for eggs. Learn how to build your household furniture, or if that doesn't interest you, brew some beer. The bottom line is this: Be a producer, not a consumer.

Finances

Proverbs 22:7 says, "…the borrower becomes the lender's slave." You need to live below your means. The truth of this proverb becomes readily apparent when you have racked up debt and you realize the only way you can pay your bills is if you stay in the military. Do not put yourself into that situation. If you are in that situation, you need to make some major changes in your life. Some repenting is probably a good place to start, then cut the fat. Sell the car for a less expensive one if you need to. Sell the house and move into a smaller one if needed. Bring your lunch to work. Stop making yourself a slave. Now that you are living below your means, start putting together your emergency fund in case you must leave the military.

One side note: There is a chance that you will be told you have to take leave as the waiver is processed or else you must comply, which may go against your conscience. Your leave is like money in the bank; don't just use it because it is sitting there. Work toward maxing out what you can roll over into the next fiscal year, then use the excess.

Conclusion

The prophet Isaiah said, "Woe to those who go down to Egypt for help and rely on horses, and trust in chariots because they are many and in horsemen because they are very strong, but they do not look to the Holy One of Israel, nor seek the LORD" (31:1). There are many practical and godly things you can be doing to harden your defenses and to make your family more durable. We all should be living wisely in accordance with God's Word daily. However, life can be messy, and there is a good chance you are not as "antifragile" as you would like to be. That should not keep you from being obedient to God though. We should not say, "I will only fight if it costs me nothing." Seek the Lord and serve Him with fear and trembling.

Bibliography

1. Groves, Rory. *Durable Trades: Family-Centered Economies That Have Stood the Test of Time*. Eugene, OR: Front Porch Republic Books, 2020.
2. New American Standard Bible, 1995.

6

When Things Go South

The world is a battlefield, and there are casualties and wounds in battle, but the battle is the Lord's and its end is victory. To attempt an escape from the battle is to flee from the liabilities of warfare against sinful men for battle with an angry God. To face the battle is to suffer the penalties of man's wrath and the blessing of God's grace and law.

— RJ Rushdoony: The Institutes of Biblical Law (668)

IN THE GOSPEL OF LUKE WHEN JESUS IS TALKING about discipleship, he mentions counting the cost prior to starting to build a tower (14:28). This isn't an argument for us to just give up, to throw in the towel. This isn't a justification for not following Jesus. Instead, "Beloved, do not be surprised at the fiery ordeal among you, which comes upon you for your testing..." (1 Peter 4:12). You should expect being obedient to Christ will cost something, maybe a job in the military...even your life. The thought of laying down your life for the things you love should not be foreign to you, as you are in the military... how much more so for Jesus Christ.

There is a real possibility that you may lose your job in the military. I pray that as you were preparing for battle, this was one of the contingencies you planned for. Take heart though, for Christ has already won the defeating blow in His death, burial, resurrection, and ascension; the war is already won. What we see and deal with today are merely the mopping-up operations as Christ's kingdom grows and the great commission is fulfilled.

Military Appeals

If a religious accommodation is denied either in part or in full, it can be appealed. Each service may have a slightly different process, but in general according to DoDI 1300.17 para 3.2.f, "Appeals will be sent to an official in the chain of command or chain of supervision above the officer or official who took final action on the request." The military appeal process stops at the secretary of your particular military department.

Military Options

If you have pursued appeals and your religious accommodation request is still denied, there is the possibility to still stay in the military. The military should consider if your religious accommodation can be met if you are reassigned to a different base or if you are reclassified to another career field (e.g. DAFI 52-201 para 2.7). For example, if your current job requires you to work on the Lord's Day, the military should consider moving you to another assignment, or if for whatever reason that is not possible, they should offer to retrain you.

Voluntary Separation

If the military denies your religious freedom and all options have been exhausted, you should have the opportunity to voluntarily separate. If you have been conducting yourself like a

Christian, when this option is presented, it will be an administrative discharge and more than likely not a punitive discharge. Even under an administrative discharge, don't let the military pull a fast one on you. Do not let them separate you with an "other than honorable" discharge just because your religious liberty is irreconcilable with the military. Hopefully they will give you an honorable discharge. The other type of separation is punitive after a court martial.

Affidavit Option

It should be stressed at this point that those going through this process should be regularly seeking counsel from the elders of their church, from the beginning to the end. Do not forget Proverbs 24:6: "For by wise guidance you will wage war, and in abundance of counselors there is victory."

You have the option to disobey an unlawful order and submit an affidavit to the commander who is causing you harm. This opens the door to the legal system. Perhaps this would get you an audience with the Supreme Court to discuss where liberty comes from.

I will leave you with this to wrestle through with your elders: If Daniel had been given the option to "voluntarily separate" from Babylon when he received the order not to pray, would he have separated or would he have still gone up to his room, opened his windows, and worshiped the Triune God? I think he would have still worshiped. But keep in mind, that doesn't necessitate you go to the den of lions. Talk to your elders. Be shrewd as serpents and innocent as doves (Matthew 10:16).

Bibliography

1. Department of Defense Instruction (DoDI) 1300.17. *Religious Liberty in the Military Services.* September 1, 2020.
2. Department of the Air Force Instruction (DAFI) 52-201. *Religious Freedom in the Department of the Air Force.* 23 June 2021.
3. Rushdoony, Rousas John. *The Institutes of Biblical Law.* The Craig Press, 1973.

Appendix A: Women in the Military

If the Church had not completely forgotten that liturgy is warfare, she would never had entertained the horrible notion that women should be ministers. What man sends his wife, daughter, mother, or sister into the front lines of battle? No real man would ever do that. But since the Church has abandoned her calling to wrestle with God on behalf of the world, since she has abandoned liturgical warfare, she has become exclusively a nurturing institution, and hence a logical place for female leadership, whether those females are women or wimpy men.

– James B. Jordan

YOU PROBABLY REALIZED THAT THE PRECEDING chapters sound like they are addressed to men. That is because they are. Women should not be "fighting in the forces which guard our country and our way of life." Now…if this book isn't currently on fire after the last sentence…we will consider a few passages from the Old Covenant and then briefly look at biblical sexuality.

Man's Clothing

> A woman shall not wear **man's [geber, not ish] clothing [keli, not silmat]**, nor shall a man put on a woman's [ishsha] clothing [silmat]; for whoever does these things is an abomination to the LORD your God. (Deuteronomy 22:5)

In this passage, the English translation seems to give a command to men and the corresponding command to women. It seems so simple: Men, don't wear woman's clothing; women, don't wear man's clothing. But it is a little more nuanced than that. You would expect if it were as simple as stated above, the word used for "man" would be *ish* rather than *geber*, and the word used for "clothing" would be *silmat* rather than *keli*. This change in the Hebrew from using the normal terms for "men's clothing" should draw our attention. What does *keli geber* (men's clothing) mean? In the Strong's definition, *keli* would be a sort of apparatus such as a weapon, utensil, vessel, or other implement. For *geber*, Strong's definition is a valiant man or warrior. What is a warrior's apparatus? It is his sword, his armor, his helmet. In this verse, you see God commanding women not to wear warrior's gear, your battle rattle, your assault gear. It doesn't get much clearer than that. It is an abomination to the Lord for a woman to don a warrior's gear.

The Lord's Army

In this section, we will briefly look at two passages. First, in the wilderness of Sinai, two years after God had rescued His people out of Egypt, God commanded the organization of Israel into armies. It is clear from this passage that the armies were to be comprised of men 20 years old and up.

> Take a census of all the congregation of the sons of Israel, by
> their families, by their fathers' households, according to the
> number of names, every male, head by head from twenty years
> old and upward, whoever is able to go out to war in Israel, you
> and Aaron shall number them by their armies. (Numbers 1:2–3)

In the second passage, Moses is giving his sermon on the
Laws of Warfare (Deuteronomy 20:5–8). He commands the offi-
cers in the army to address the men and give them the reason by
which they are excused from fighting. The first is if they built a
new house and had not yet dedicated it. Second is a man who
planted a vineyard and has not yet used its fruits. Third, if a
man is engaged but has not yet married a woman. Last, if there
is a man who is afraid or fainthearted. Each of these uses the
masculine noun for man.

The argument could just stop here, as it is very clear.
However, the counterargument can be made that these passages
would only prohibit military jobs that require a woman to don
warrior's gear and fight. Some may say that this still allows
women into the military to work as nurses, in finance, or some
other noncombatant role. Perhaps there are some circumstances
where this is true and not sinful. Either way, it should not be
the norm. In order to establish this, we will briefly look at
biblical sexuality.

Biblical Sexuality

Biblical sexuality has resurfaced as a hot topic in current theo-
logical discussion. Men like Aaron Renn, Michael Foster, Bnonn
Tennant, Zachary Garris, and Alister Roberts have been
addressing the issue through books, blogs, and articles. Twenty
years ago, before it was popular, pastors like Douglas Wilson
were addressing the roles of men and women as found in Scripture. Stephen B. Clark's 1980 work titled *Man and Woman in*

Christ: An Examination of the Roles of Men and Women in Light of Scripture and the Social Sciences has been republished in 2021. It is considered one of the most important works on biblical sexuality.

The findings aren't revolutionary or mind-blowing. The findings are obvious to everyone who is not suppressing the truth in unrighteousness (Romans 1:18). Men and women are different. This is obvious from Scripture and by simple observation. God created man to be strong, to protect and provide (Genesis 2:15). He created man to exercise dominion, to subdue and fill the earth (Genesis 1:26–28). God created woman to be man's helper (Genesis 2:18). This isn't derogatory. We have the same worth and value before God, but God did create men and women with different roles or functions. The following looks at biblical sexuality from a narrow angle, from the angle of fighting. God created women to bear seed. Men were created to fight.

For, men we will zero in on the word used in Genesis 2:15 for *keep*. This word may be better understood as to *guard* the Garden of Eden, in a similar way that the Levitical priests were to guard the temple. Adam as the priest was to guard the garden from the outside world. Adam was to protect the garden sanctuary and his wife from the dragon or serpent. As we know, he failed in this task, and the dragon was allowed entrance to the garden and allowed to deceive Adam's wife, Eve. The argument that men are to protect can be made from Scripture post-fall quite easily, but for the purposes of this section, we will stop at God's intention from creation.

As seen in Genesis 2:18, woman was created to be a helper to man. One of women's greatest tasks is to bear children, to help Adam be fruitful and multiply. Although this is not the only role of women (e.g., see Proverbs 31), it is an important one. We can see this in strange passages like 1 Timothy 2:15: "But women will be preserved through the bearing of children..." The context the apostle Paul gives when he says that is the Garden of Eden, as Adam and Eve are being tempted. To understand what is going on, we must start with God cursing the dragon. In Genesis 3:15, God says, "And I will put enmity between you and the woman, and between your seed and her seed; he shall bruise you on the head, and you shall bruise him on the heel." It is through the woman's seed that God will bring salvation to the world; that promised seed will crush the head of the dragon. This theme is seen throughout Scripture in David crushing Goliath's head, Jael crushing Sisera's head, and the unnamed woman crushing Abimelech's head, and so forth. This promise from Genesis 3:15 is fulfilled in Jesus Christ on the cross. Jesus, the seed of the woman, crushed Satan's (the dragon's) head at Golgotha (the place of the skull), bringing salvation. But the story does not stop here. The story of the woman's seed continues to this day. Romans 16:20 says, "The God of peace will soon crush Satan under your feet." Women's task in working to build and fight for God's kingdom is largely through childbearing.

It seems so obvious, but to draw this out a little further, you can see that form follows function. If the preceding statements are true (which they are), you should see this in how God created man and woman. Men were created to fight, to work the ground, to protect; they were created strong. Women were created to nurture and to be a life giver; they were created with a womb and breasts. These differences do not make one better than the other. These differences are good and should be celebrated, not scorned. In considering women in the military, we should not rebel against God's created design. If there is anything, not just some noncombatant job in the military, that is keeping a woman from being primarily focused toward the home, it should be abandoned.

Appendix B: Other Religions in the Military

The real object of the First Amendment was not to countenance, much less to advance, Mahomedanism [Islam], or Judaism, or infidelity, by prostrating Christianity; but to exclude all rivalry among Christian sects, and to prevent any national ecclesiastical establishment which should give to an hierarchy the exclusive patronage of the national government. It thus cut off the means of religious persecution (the vice and pest of former ages), and of the subversion of the rights of conscience in matters of religion which had been trampled upon almost from the days of the Apostles to the present age....Probably at the time of the adoption of the Constitution, and the first amendment to it...the general, if not the universal, sentiment in America was that Christianity ought to receive encouragement from the State, so far as was not incompatible with the previous rights of conscience and the freedom of religious worship. An attempt to level all religions and to make it a matter of state policy to hold all in utter indifference would have created universal disapprobation, if not universal indignation.

– Joseph Story (1779-1845), Associate Justice of the United State Supreme Court, Commentaries on the Constitution of the United States, sections 1871, 1868

RELIGIOUS LIBERTY IS A CHRISTIAN VIRTUE AND ONLY a Christian virtue. As we saw in the opening chapter of this field manual, liberty, in general, only comes as a fruit from the gospel of Jesus Christ. Anything apart from the law of the Triune God leads to tyranny. This includes any other named religion and the religion of secular humanism. It is readily apparent that civilizations that have flourished had their roots in Christianity. But what happens when you kill those roots? We are seeing it now; the tree begins to die...liberty wanes. We see some semblance of a tree, but it will eventually topple.

R. J. Rushdoony, in his *Chalcedon Position Paper No. 31*, written in 1982, examines the topic of religious liberty verses religious toleration. The First Amendment at its inception was an incredible victory for true religious liberty; the state could not regulate how Christians were to worship and exercise their faith in Jesus Christ. But religious liberty is now dead in the United States, and what we have is religious toleration. Rushdoony states, "In religious toleration, the state is paramount, and, in every sphere, its powers are totalitarian. The state is the sovereign or lord, the supreme religious entity or power. The state decrees what and who can exist, and it establishes the terms of existence. The state reserves the power to license and tolerate one or more religions upon its own conditions and subject to state controls, regulation, and supervision" (pg. 147).

This should bring to mind the topic of *compelling justification* discussed in chapter 3. The state currently believes it reserves the right to infringe on religious liberty if there is a compelling justification. Another way of saying this is that the state believes the Church is subordinate to the civil government. This makes the secular humanism of the state the ultimate religion of the land. It is the preferred religion. Without the Triune God as the foundation of our society, what is tolerated will become narrower and narrower. Psalm 127:1 says, "Unless the LORD builds the house, they labor in vain who build it." Any attempt to build something apart from the Creator to the heavens and the earth is a dead venture; it is suicidal.

What should Christians do about other religions in the military? The answer is simple: nothing. Other religions in the military are not the root of the problem, but the outworking of a pluralistic society. It should be expected that the shadows of different religions are seen in the military as secular humanism rules supreme in our society. You can believe whatever you want, as long as you ultimately bend the knee to Caesar. That seems to sidestep the issue, but it doesn't. Practically speaking, Christians need to worship God faithfully, they need to know their Bibles, they need to be involved in the community around them and in local politics, and they need to ensure the gospel is not confined to their heads and hearts. In other words, they need to live as if Christ is King of kings and Lord of lords.

Rushdoony concludes his position paper as follows:

What is increasingly apparent is that the triune God of Scripture, the Bible itself, and all faith grounded thereon, are contrary to public policy. Christianity has no place in our state schools and universities; it does not inform the councils of state; every effort by Christians to affect the political process is called a violation of the First Amendment and "the separation of church and state." Our freedom of religion is something to be tolerated only if we keep it between our two ears. A war has been declared against us, and we had better know it, and we had better stand and fight before it is too late. We may be able to live under religious toleration, but it will beget all the ancient evil of compromise, hypocrisy, and a purely or largely public religion. It will replace conscience with a state license, and freedom with a state-endowed cell of narrow limits. That is the *best* that toleration may afford us in the days ahead. But the Lord alone is God, and He does not share His throne with the State. If we surrender to Caesar, we will share in Caesar's judgment and fall. If we stand with the Lord, we shall stand in His Spirit and power. "Stand fast therefore in the liberty wherewith Christ hath made us free, and be not entangled again with the yoke of bondage" (Gal. 5:1). At the heart of the yoke of bondage is the belief and fear that the powers of man (and the state) are greater than the power of God. It is bondage to believe that man can prevail, or that man can frustrate God's sovereign and holy purpose. The only real question is this: will we be part of the world's defeat and judgment, or a part of the Lord's Kingdom and victory?

As far as the other religions, they will eventually topple to the gospel of Jesus Christ. Christ is victorious, and His kingdom will grow. This is not accomplished through the sword, but through the preaching and outworking of the gospel within our society. As Christ's kingdom grows, the military will eventually mirror society, and the discussion of other religions in the military will be moot.

Bibliography

1. Rushdoony, Rousas John. *The Roots of Reconstruction.* Vallecito, CA: Ross House Books, 1991.
2. Story, Joseph, LL.D. *Commentaries on the Constitution of the United States in Three Volumes (1833).* Lonang Institute, 2005.